MW00956031

This Notebook Belongs To:

Subject:

Instructor:

Location:

Date:

Cool Notebooks

Made in the USA
Monee, IL
01 March 2022

92097842R00057